IMPORTANT FACTS ABOUT YOUR HEALTH

Science Book 3rd Grade

Children's Biology Books

In this book, we're going to talk about important health facts. So, let's get right to it!

Staying healthy is easier if you do some things the right way every day. Suppose you want to change a bad habit. If you do something the right way every day for 30 days, you can form a new good habit. Here are some important factors you need to work on to stay healthy.

Most people who form these good habits early in life stay healthy for a long time.

- ➪ Get enough sleep every night.
- ➪ Eat healthy foods and drink enough water.
- ➪ Get enough exercise.

GETTING ENOUGH SLEEP

Everybody needs to get the proper sleep at night. The amount of hours of sleep you need depends on your age. For example, for kids from age 5 to age 10, about 10 hours of sleep are needed every night.

Most kids do a lot during the day. You go to school and then you might do extracurricular activities after school like sports or music. In the late afternoon, you might go out with friends, feed or play with your pets, do chores around the house, or finish your homework. At night, you might be playing or working on your computer or texting on your phone. All of these things you do take a huge amount of energy. You need sleep at night so your body and mind can rest and get ready for the next day that's filled with activities!

WHY GETTING ENOUGH SLEEP IS IMPORTANT

In addition to giving your body and mind rest for the next day, sleep is important for other reasons too. Scientists are still studying all the things your body and mind do when they are asleep. While you're sleeping your brain sorts through the information that you were gathering during the day and stores it, almost like a filing cabinet in your mind.

The cells in your brain replace the chemicals they need to function properly. You even work on problems during your dreams. Most kids who need at least 10 or 11 hours of sleep every night are only getting about 9.5 hours of sleep a night. If you're only getting 9.5 hours every night and you really need 11 that means by the end of the year, you're getting 547.5 hours less sleep than you should have!

You should be able to tell if you haven't had enough sleep because you'll feel tired during the day. You might be kind of cranky and not able to think too clearly either. If you're fighting with one of your best friends over something stupid or you can't follow directions easily, it might mean you're deprived of sleep too.

Maybe you're usually good at math, but tonight's homework seems impossible or you feel awkward playing a sport that you're usually really good at. These can be clues that you're not getting enough sleep.

If you're worried about getting taller, you should sleep more too. Scientists believe that too little sleep can stunt your growth. Your immune system can be compromised too, if you don't get enough sleep. That just means you might get sick or catch colds more often. If you think you're not getting enough sleep, here are some tips you can try:

Go to bed at the same time every single night. It helps your body anticipate sleeping.

About 30 minutes before bedtime,
do something calming like taking a
bath or reading your favorite book.

Soda

Don't drink sodas or iced tea or other drinks that have caffeine in them before bedtime.

Just use your bed for sleep, not for homework, reading, or chatting on the phone. You need to associate your bed with sleep!

Scared child watching scary movie on tv

Don't watch scary television programs or movies before bed. They sometimes stay in your mind, which makes it difficult to sleep.

If you have a TV in your room, turn it off a half hour before it's bedtime. Studies have shown that if you have a television in your room, you're sleeping less than kids who don't have a television set in their rooms.

young boy turning off the television

EATING HEALTHY FOODS

Most people know what foods are healthy for them, but they still don't eat properly. Even if you're not ill and you don't eat properly, you can feel ill. Your body needs the correct nutrition to function properly.

Breakfast is a really important meal because it gives you the energy that you need to be active all day long. Kids should choose breakfast foods that are high in carbohydrates, but low in sugar. A bowl of cereal that's low in sugar, slices of whole grain toast, or a bowl of oatmeal are all good choices. Yogurt that's low in sugar mixed with fresh fruit is another good choice. It's good to have protein like eggs or sausage once in a while too. Protein helps you stay full until lunchtime and also helps your muscles get strong.

CHOOSE VEGETABLES WITH DARK COLORS

Most of us don't eat enough vegetables. Your body needs about 2 cups of vegetables and 2 cups of fruits every day. If you don't get these servings of vegetables and fruits, there's a good chance you're not getting enough vitamins and minerals. Leafy, dark vegetables are filled with vitamin A, vitamin C, vitamin K and folate, all of which are vital for good health.

These dark veggies also contain iron, which is very important in making healthy red blood cells. They contain calcium, which is crucial for strong teeth and bones. The fiber that you eat when you get enough vegetables helps your intestines work properly so you can go to the bathroom easily.

broccoli
spinach
kale
arugul
chard leaves
lettuce

Make sure you get some of these "superhero" vegetables into your diet:

Broccoli

Spinach

Kale

Arugula

Swiss Chard

Romaine Lettuce

CHOOSE HEALTHY FRUITS FOR SWEETNESS

Most people love sweet foods, but too many sugary treats will quickly make you gain weight and they have no nutrients to keep you healthy. When you're craving something sweet, a treat of fruit is much healthier. Oranges, other citrus fruits, and strawberries have tons of vitamin C to boost your immunity to illnesses. Blueberries and other dark berries have antioxidants, which help your body fight off serious diseases, such as cancer. Apples have lots of fiber to keep your intestines healthy.

acai berries
strawberries
blueberries
cherries
bananas
apples

Add these amazing, sweet-tasting fruits to your diet:

Acai Berries

Strawberries

Blueberries

Cherries

Bananas

Apples

CHOOSE WHOLE GRAINS

When you eat breads and cereals, choose whole grains instead of products made with white flour. They're healthier for you because they have fiber and more nutrients than products made with white flour.

DRINK PLENTY OF WATER

It's hard to believe this, but the tissues in our bodies are actually made up of 50-65% water. When we exercise or just enjoy basking in the sun outdoors, our bodies sweat and release water. When we're thirsty, our bodies are calling out for us to replenish them with clear, cool water. It's the healthiest way to quench our thirst.

It has no calories and is completely free of sugar. If you like drinking something with taste, put some cut-up fruit in your water or a squeeze of lemon or lime. We need about 5-8 glasses of water every day. In addition to quenching our thirst, water also helps flush out toxins.

GETTING ENOUGH EXERCISE

At school you sit most of the day and at home sometimes you're playing video games or working on the computer or doing your homework. All these activities are "sedentary," which simply means you're sitting instead of moving around. You need to run, bike, swim, or play a sport every day for at least 30 minutes. Lots of kids are overweight because they aren't active enough during the day.

If you don't like sports, that's ok. Just find something you like to do that's active. You can take your dog out for a walk and just walk briskly for 30 minutes. Some kids like to take classes in karate, dancing, or skating. There are so many different activities that will get you off the couch and moving around. Find something fun that you like to do and it will help you stay slim and strong.

SUMMARY

Good health is important so you have the energy to do the things you love to do. To keep yourself healthy, you need to sleep enough hours every night. You also need to eat healthy foods and stay away from those that aren't healthy. Our bodies are mostly made of water so drinking enough water every day keeps our bodies hydrated. Exercising every day is very important too, so you can keep your muscles strong and burn off the calories you eat. If you're not doing these things now, try to change your bad habits into good ones by doing something new for 30 days in a row.

Awesome! Now that you know more about important health facts you may want to read about what happens when you're sick or have an injury in the Baby Professor book What Happens During an Emergency? Emergency Book for Kids.